SIXTY-MINUTE SHAKESPEARE

A MIDSUMMER NIGHT'S DREAM

by Cass Foster

SIXTY-MINUTE SHAKESPEARE

A MIDSUMMER NIGHT'S DREAM

by Cass Foster

from A MIDSUMMER NIGHT'S DREAM
by WILLIAM SHAKESPEARE

published by
Five Star Publications, Inc.
Chandler, Arizona

Linda F. Radke, President
Five Star Publications, Inc.
P.O. Box 6698
Chandler, AZ 85246-6698
(480) 940-8182
www.FiveStarPublications.com

FIVE STAR
PUBLICATIONS
Shining Brightly Since 1985

For performance rights please contact:
Dramatic Publishing
www.DramaticPublishing.com
(800) 448-7469

www.GetShakespeare.com

Publisher's Cataloging-In-Publication Data
Shakespeare, William, 1564-1616.
A midsummer night's dream I (abridged) by Cass Foster.- 1st ed.
   p. em.- (Classics for all ages) (The Sixty-Minute Shakespeare)
Summary: A condensed version of Shakespeare's play about the strange events that take place in a forest inhabited by fairies who magically transform the romantic fate of two young couples.
ISBN: 1-877749-37-0
ISBN-13: 978-1-877749-37-7
eISBN: 978-1-58985-186-3
   1. Man-woman relationships- Greece -Athens- Drama (1. Plays)
I. Cass Foster, 1948- . II. Title. III. Series.   IV. Scenes:
Foster, Cass, 1948- Sixty-Minute Shakespeare.
PR2827. A25 1997   97-24577
822.3'3-dc21   CIP   AC

Electronic edition provided by:

eStarPublish.com
The eBook Division of Five Star Publications, Inc.

Printed in the United States of America

Book Design: Barbara Kordesh
Copy Editor: Paul M. Howey
Editor, Sixth Edition: Gary E. Anderson

To Mom

Thanks for everything

Actor / Director Notes

Welcome to
THE SIXTY-MINUTE SHAKESPEARE

Thanks to the progressive thinking of so many curriculum developers, Language Arts people and the splendid film work being done by directors such as Kenneth Branagh and Franco Zeffrelli, there has been a phenomenal growth in interest in Shakespeare.

No playwright, past or present, approaches the brilliance and magnitude of William Shakespeare. What other individual has even come close to understanding and then dramatizing the human condition? Just for the fun of it, I am listing (following these introductory remarks) a sample of themes and images so richly developed in the canon of his plays.

Shakespeare's characters are so well-rounded and beautifully constructed that it is common to see them as actual historical figures. When someone mentions Hamlet, Iago, Ophelia, or Puck, we immediately experience images and emotions that come from memories of people we know. We may feel compassion, frustration, sorrow, or pleasure.

As one of the wealthiest people of his times, Shakespeare earned his living as a playwright, theatre manager, actor, and shareholder in the Globe Theatre. He worked tirelessly to entertain. (Theatres presented a new play every day and the average new play had a total of only ten performances over an entire season.) He rebelled against the contemporary theatrical standards (the neo-classical principles that limited dramatic structure throughout France and Italy), he took plots from other published works (making them uniquely his own), and he created a spectacle (without the use of elaborate scenery) to captivate audiences of all social levels.

Imagine the challenge in quieting a crowd of three thousand in a theatre where vendors sell wine, beer, ale, nuts, and cards; where there is no intermission; where birds fly overhead; and where audience members stand near performers. Such was the setting in which Shakespeare's plays were originally staged.

The world's most familiar and successful wordsmith used language to skillfully create images, plot, and a sense of music and rhythm. The purpose behind this series is to reduce (not contemporize) the language. The unabridged Shakespeare simply isn't practical in all situations. Not all educators or directors have the luxury of time to explore the entire text. This is not intended to be a substitute for a thorough study of Shakespeare. It is merely a stepping stone.

I challenge each of you to go beyond the *Sixty-Minute* versions. Use the comfort, appreciation, and self-confidence you will gain to go further. Be proud of the insights and knowledge you acquire, but do not be satisfied. The more you read, the more you gain.

May each of you be blessed with an abundance of good health and happiness. I thank you for your interest in our work and hope you are are pleased with what we have done.

May the Verse Be With You!

A COUPLE OF STAGING CONSIDERATIONS

Scenery

There are two excellent reasons theatres rarely use much scenery when staging Shakespeare. The first is related to the number of changes required. If we have to wait every five to ten minutes to watch scenery struck and set up, we end up watching a play about moving lumber. The second is because the audience will lose sight of what the play is about. Audiences need a couple minutes to adjust to the new scenic look of a dazzling waterfall and lush forest. By the time they take it all in and start paying attention to what the actors are saying, it is time to set up the next scene and the audience will be lost.

Location is normally established through dialogue and the use of a few simple props: a throne-like chair for the king's court, a long table with benches for an inn, or a bed for the queen's bed chamber. The key is to keep it simple.

Pacing

You will want to keep things moving all the time. That doesn't mean actors should talk and move quickly; it simply means one scene should flow smoothly to the next without delay or interruption.

As Scene One ends, the actors pick up their props and walk off. Actors for Scene Two enter from a different direction with their props and begin dialogue as soon as they enter the acting area, putting their props in place as they speak. Yes, the audience will still have view of the actors in the first scene, but they will gladly accept this convention if it means taking fifteen minutes off performance time.

TWO HIGHLY RECOMMENDED WEB SITES

www.ShakeSpirit.com

A revolutionary site offering Shakespeare gifts,
teaching assistance, resources and quotes.

www.ShakespeareLRC.com

SHAKESPEARE LEARNING RESOURCE CENTER.
Free Library Dedicated to Shakespeare
and the Performing and Visual Arts.

IMAGES AND THEMES TO LOOK FOR
IN THE VARIOUS PLAYS

Mistaken identity

Wisdom of fools

Insanity

Greed and corruption

Religious persecution

The elements

The supernatural

Darkness and light

Loneliness or isolation

Anti-Semitism

Conspiracy

Revenge

Hypocrisy

Abandonment

Pride

Honor

Violence

Bravery

Rebellion

Savagery

Seduction

Disease or physical decay

Loyalty

War

Marriage

False accusations

Irresponsible power

Destiny or fate

Real or pretended madness

Ambition

Tyranny

Foils or opposites

Spying

Paranoia

Play-acting

Justice

Heavenly retribution

Forgiveness

Witchcraft

Mortality

Self-destruction

Black or white magic

Animals

Nature

Reality vs. illusion

Astrological influence

Characters reforming

Old age

Freedom

Usurping of power

Fertility suppression

Sexual misadventure

Melancholy

Corrupt society

Love and/or friendship

Multiple meanings of words

Thought vs. action

Impetuous love

Role of women

Human frailty

Preparing for leadership

Charity/Betrayal

THE COMPLETE WORKS
OF WILLIAM SHAKESPEARE

1589 - 1591	Henry VI, Part 1, 2 and 3
1592 - 1593	Richard III
1593 - 1594	Titus Andronicus
1592 - 1594	Comedy of Errors
1593 - 1594	Taming of the Shrew
1594	The Two Gentlemen of Verona
1594 - 1595	Love's Labor's Lost
1594 - 1596	King John
1595	Richard II
1595 - 1596	A Midsummer Night's Dream
1595 - 1596	Romeo and Juliet
1596 - 1597	The Merchant of Venice
1597	The Merry Wives of Windsor
1597 - 1598	Henry IV, Part 1 and 2
1598 - 1599	Much Ado About Nothing
1599	Henry V
1599	Julius Caesar
1599	As You Like It
1600 - 1601	Hamlet
1601 - 1602	Twelfth Night
1601 - 1602	Troilus and Cressida
1602 - 1603	All's Well That Ends Well
1604	Measure for Measure
1604	Othello
1605	The Tragedy of King Lear
1606	Macbeth
1606 - 1607	Antony and Cleopatra
1607 - 1608	Timon of Athens
1607 - 1608	Pericles, Prince of Tyre
1607 - 1608	Coriolanus
1609- 1610	Cymbeline
1609 - 1610	The Winter's Tale
1611	The Tempest
1612 - 1613	Henry VIII
1613	Two Noble Kinsmen (Authorship in question)

23 April 1564 - 23 April 1616

*"If we wish to know the force of human genius,
we should read Shakespeare. If we wish to see the
insignificance of human learning, we may study
his commentators."*

William Hazlitt (1778-1830) English Essayist. "On the Ignorance of the
Learned," in *Edinburgh Magazine* (July 1818).

COMMON QUOTES FROM THE BARD

Romeo and Juliet

> Parting is such sweet sorrow.
> A plague o' both your houses.
> O Romeo, Romeo! Wherefore art thou Romeo?

A Midsummer Night's Dream

> Lord, what fools these mortals be.
> The course of true love never did run smooth.
> To say the truth, reason and love keep little company together now-a-days.

As You Like It

> All that glisters is not gold.
> Love is blind.
> All the world's a stage
> And all the men and women merely players.
> For ever and a day.

Twelfth Night

> Some are born great, some achieve greatness, and some have greatness thrust upon them.
> Out of the jaws of death.
> O, had I but followed the arts!
> Many a good hanging prevents a bad marriage.

Henry IV, Part 1

> The better part of valor is discretion.
> To give the devil his due.
> He hath eaten me out of house and home.

Henry VI, Part 2

> Let's kill all the lawyers.

The Merry Wives of Windsor

> Better three hours too soon than a minute too late.

Casablanca

> This could be the start of a beautiful friendship.

Macbeth

> Out, damned spot. Out, I say!
> Screw your courage to the sticking place.

Hamlet

> Something is rotten in the state of Denmark.
> To be or not to be. That is the question.
> The lady doth protest too much, methinks.
> Good night, sweet prince, And flights of
>   angels sing thee to thy rest!

The Merchant of Venice

> The devil can cite scriptures for his purpose.

Pericles

> Few love to hear the sins they love to act.

Richard III

> Now is the winter of our discontent.
> Off with his head!
> A horse! A horse! My kingdom for a horse.

Julius Caesar

> Beware the ides of March.
> Friends, Romans, countrymen, lend me your ears.
> It was Greek to me.

Much Ado About Nothing

> The world must be peopled. When I said I would die a
>   bachelor, I did not think I should live till I were married.

Measure for Measure

> The miserable have no other medicine but only hope.

Troilus and Cressida

> To fear the worst oft cures the worse.

The Comedy of Errors

> Unquiet meals make ill digestions.

Cast of Characters

Theseus, Duke of Athens
Egeus, father of Hermia
Lysander, in love with Hermia
Demetrius, in love with Hermia
Philostrate, Master of Revels to Theseus

Peter Quince, a carpenter; Prologue in the play
Snug, the joiner; Lion in the play
Nick Bottom, a weaver; Pyramus in the play
Francis Flute, a bellows mender; Thisby in the play
Tom Snout, a tinker; Wall in the play
Robin Starveling, a tailor; Moonshine in the play

Hippolyta, Queen of the Amazons, betrothed to Theseus
Hermia, daughter to Egeus, in love with Lysander
Helena, in love with Demetrius

Oberon, King of the Fairies
Titania, Queen of the Fairies
Puck, or Robin Goodfellow
Peaseblossom, Fairy
Cobweb, Fairy
Moth, Fairy
Mustardseed, Fairy
Other fairies if desired

Place
Athens and a wood near it

ACT I, SCENE 1.
THE PALACE OF THESEUS.

Enter Theseus and Hippolyta.

Theseus. Now, fair Hippolyta, our nuptial hour
    Draws on apace. Four happy days bring in
    Another moon but O methinks, how slow
    This old moon wanes! She lingers° my desires,
    Like a stepdame, or a dowager,
    Long withering out diminishes a young man's revenue.°

Hippolyta. Four days will quickly steep themselves in
    night,
    Four nights will quickly dream away the time;
    And then the moon, like to a silver bow new-bent in
    heaven, shall behold the night
    Of our solemnities.

Theseus. Hippolyta, I wooed thee with my sword,°
    And won thy love, doing thee injuries;
    But I will wed thee in another key,
    With pomp, with triumph, and with reveling.

Enter Egeus, Hermia, Lysander and Demetrius.

Egeus. Happy be Theseus, our renowned Duke!

Theseus. Thanks, good Egeus. What's the news with thee?

Lingers: delays.   *Long withering out:* diminishes his money (to support her)
Sword: captured Hippolyta by conquering the Amazons.

Egeus. Full of vexation come I, with complaint
Against my child, my daughter Hermia.
Stand forth, Demetrius. My noble Lord,
This man hath my consent to marry her.
Stand forth, Lysander. And, my gracious Duke
This man hath bewitched the bosom of my child.
Thou, thou, Lysander, thou hast given her rhymes,
And interchanged love tokens with my child.
I beg the ancient privilege of Athens:
As she is mine, I may dispose of her,
Which shall be either to this gentleman
Or to her death, according to our law
Immediately° provided in that case.

Theseus. What say you, Hermia? Be advised, fair maid.
To you, your father should be as a god.
Demetrius is a worthy gentleman.

Hermia. So is Lysander.

Theseus. But in this kind, wanting your father's voice,° the
other must be held the worthier.

Hermia. I beseech your Grace that I may know
The worst that may befall me in this case,
If I refuse to wed Demetrius.

Theseus. Either to die the death, or to abjure forever the
society of men. For aye, to be in a shady cloister mewed,°
To live a barren sister all your life.

Hermia. So I will grow, so live, so die, my lord.

Immediately: expressly.   *Voice:* approval.   *Mewed:* caged.

2

Theseus. Take time to pause; and, by the next new moon...
   The sealing day betwixt my love and me,
   For everlasting bond of fellowship...
   Upon that day either prepare to die
   For disobedience to your father's will,
   Or else to wed Demetrius, as he would,
   Or on Diana's alter to protest
   For aye austerity and single life.

Exit Egeus, Hippolyta and Theseus.

Demetrius. Relent, sweet Hermia. And, Lysander, yield
   Thy crazèd title° to my certain right.

Lysander. You have her father's love, Demetrius;
   Let me have Hermia's. Do you marry him.

Demetrius exits.

Lysander. How now, my love! Why is your cheek so pale?
   How chance° the roses there do fade so fast?

Hermia. Belike ° for want of rain, which I could well bring
   forth from the tempest of my eyes.

Lysander. Aye me! For aught that I could ever read,
   Could ever hear by tale or history,
   The course of true love never did run smooth.

Hermia. Oh hell! To choose love by another's eyes!

Crazed title: flawed claim.   *How chance:* How does it come that?
Belike: perhaps.

3

Lysander. Hear me, Hermia.
   I have a widow aunt, a dowager
   Of great revenue, and she hath no child.
   From Athens is her house remote seven leagues,
   And she respects me as her only son.
   There, gentle Hermia, may I marry thee
   And to that place the sharp Athenian law
   Cannot pursue us. If thou lovest me, then,
   Steal forth thy father's house tomorrow night;
   And in the wood, a league without the town,
   Where I did meet thee once with Helena,
   To do observance to a morn of May,
   There will I stay for thee.

Hermia. My good Lysander!
   I swear to thee, by Cupid's strongest bow,
   By his best arrow with the golden head°
   In that same place thou hast appointed me,
   Tomorrow truly will I meet with thee.

Lysander. Keep promise, love.

Lysander exits and Helena enters from another direction.

Hermia. G-d° speed fair Helena! Wither away?

Helena. Call you me fair? That fair again unsay.
   Demetrius loves your fair. ° O happy fair!

Golden head: Cupid's arrows with golden heads caused love, leaden ones
caused dislike.   *Fair:* beauty.

Helena. O, teach me how you look.

Hermia. I frown upon him, yet he loves me still.

Helena. O that your frowns would teach my smiles such
  skill.

Hermia. I give him curses, yet he gives me love.

Helena. O that my prayers could such affection move!

Hermia. The more I hate, the more he follows me.

Helena. The more I love, the more he hateth me.

Hermia. Take comfort. He no more shall see my face;
  Lysander and myself will fly this place.
  In the wood, where often you and I
  Upon faint primrose bed were wont to lie,
  Emptying of our bosoms of their counsel sweet,
  There my Lysander and myself shall meet.
  Farewell, sweet playfellow. Pray thou for us,
  And good luck grant thee thy Demetrius! (*Exit Hermia.*)

Helena. Through Athens I am thought as fair as she. But
  what of that? Demetrius thinks not so. I will go tell
  Demetrius of fair Hermia's flight. Then to the wood will
  he tomorrow night pursue her; and for this intelligence°
  If I have thanks, it is a dear expense: ° But herein mean I
  to enrich my pain, To have his sight thither and back
  again. (*She exits.*)

Intelligence: piece of news.   *Expense:* heavy cost gladly incurred.

ACT I, SCENE 2.
QUINCE'S HOUSE.

Enter Quince, Snug, Bottom, Flute, Snout and Starveling.

Quince. Is all our company here?

Bottom. You were best to call them individually, man by man, according to the scrip.

Quince. Here is the scroll of every man's name, which is thought fit, through all Athens, to play in our interlude° before the Duke and Duchess, on his wedding day at night.

Bottom. First, good Peter Quince, say what the play treats on; then read the names of the actors.

Quince. Marry,° our play is, "The most lamentable comedy, and most cruel death of Pyramus and Thisby."

Bottom. A very good piece of work, I assure you, and a merry. Now, good Peter Quince, call forth your actors by the scroll. Masters, spread yourselves.

Quince. Answer as I call you. Nick Bottom, the weaver.

Bottom. Ready. Name what part I am for, and proceed.

Quince. You, Nick Bottom, are set down for Pyramus.

Bottom. What is Pyramus? A lover, or a tyrant?

Interlude: dramatic entertainment.   *Marry:* interjection (e.g. "Good heavens.")

Quince. A lover that kills himself, most gallant, for love.

Bottom. That love will ask some tears in the true
   performing of it: if I do it, let the audience look
   to their eyes. I will move Storms. Now, name the
   rest of the players.

Quince. Francis Flute, the bellows mender.

Flute. Here, Peter Quince.

Quince. Flute, you must take Thisby on you.

Flute. What is Thisby? A wand'ring knight?

Quince. It is the lady that Pyramus must love. *(All laugh.)*

Flute. Nay, faith, let me not play a woman. I have a beard
   coming.

Quince. That's all one.° You shall play it in a mask, and you
   may speak as small as you will.

Bottom. If I may hide my face, let me play Thisby too. I'll
   speak in a monstrous little voice, *(In a deep voice.)*
   "Thisne, Thisne!" *(In a high-pitched voice.)*
   "Ah Pyramus, my lover dear! Thy Thisby
   dear, and lady dear!"

Quince. No, no. You must play Pyramus, and, Flute, you
   Thisby.

That's all one: it makes no difference.

Bottom. Well, proceed.

Quince. Robin Starveling, the tailor.

Starveling. Here, Peter Quince.

Quince. Robin Starveling, you must play Thisby's mother.
Tom Snout, the tinker.

Snout. Here, Peter Quince.

Quince. You, Pyramus' father. Myself, Thisby's father.
Snug, the joiner, you the lion's part.

Snug. Have you the lion's part written? Pray you, if it be,
give it to me, for I am slow of study.

Quince. You may do it extempore, for it is nothing but
roaring.

Bottom. Let me play the lion too. I will roar so that I will
do any man's heart good to hear me.

Quince. An you should do it too terribly, you would fright
the Duchess and the ladies.

Starveling. That would hang us, every mother's son.

Bottom. I will roar as gently as any dove. I will roar as any
nightingale.

Quince. You can play no part but Pyramus.

Bottom. Well, I will undertake it.

Quince. Masters, here are your parts; and I am to entreat
you, request you, and desire you, to con° them by
tomorrow night; and meet me in the palace wood,
a mile without the town, by moonlight. There we
will rehearse, for if we meet in the city, we shall
be dogged with company, and our devices°
known. In the meantime I will draw a will of
properties,° such as our play wants. I pray you,
fail me not.

Bottom. We will meet; and there we may rehearse most
obscenely° and courageously. Take pains, be
perfect. Adieu.

Quince. At the Duke's oak we meet.

Con: study.   *Devices:* plans.   *Properties:* stage props   *Obscenely:* he means
seemly or properly.

ACT II, SCENE 1.

A fairy enters from one side and Puck the other.

Puck. How now, spirit! Wither wander you?

Fairy. Over hill, over dale,
  Thorough bush, thorough brier,
  Over park, over pale,°
  Thorough flood, thorough fire,
  Swifter than the moon's sphere;
  And I serve the Fairy Queen,
  To dew her orbs° upon the green.
  Farewell, thou lob° of spirits; I'll be gone.
  Our Queen and all her elves come here anon.

Puck. The King doth keep his revels here tonight.
  Take heed the Queen come not within his sight.
  For Oberon is passing fell and wrath,°
  Because that she as her attendant hath
  A lovely boy, stolen from an Indian king;
  She never had so sweet a changeling.°
  And jealous Oberon would have the child
  Knight of his train, to trace° the forests wild.
  But she perforce withholds the lovèd boy,
  Crowns him with flowers, and makes him all her joy.

Fairy. Either I mistake your shape and making quite,
  Or else you are that shrewd and knavish sprite
  Called Robin Goodfellow.

Pale: enclosed park.   *Orbs:* fairy rings.   *Lob:* clumsy fellow.
Wrath: fierce and angry.   *Changeling:* a stolen child.   *Trace:* traverse.

Puck. Thou speakest aright;
  I am that merry wanderer of the night.
  I jest to Oberon, and make him smile.
  But, room, fairy, here comes Oberon.

*Enter Oberon with his train through one side and Titania,
with her train, through the other.*

Oberon. Ill met by moonlight, proud Titania.

Titania. What, jealous Oberon! Fairy, skip hence.
  I have forsworn his bed and company.

Oberon. Tarry, rash wanton;° am not I thy lord?

Titania. (Sarcastically.) Then I must be thy lady.

Oberon. Why should Titania cross her Oberon?
  I do but beg a little changeling boy,
  To be my henchman.°

Titania. Set your heart at rest.
  The fairy land buys not the child of me.
  His mother was a vot'ress° of my order,
  And, in the spicèd Indian air, by night,
  Full often hath she gossiped by my side,
  And sat with me on Neptune's yellow sands.
  She, being mortal, of that boy did die;
  And for her sake do I rear up her boy,
  And for her sake I will not part with him.

Waton: hasty, willful creature.   *Henchman:* page.
Vot'ress: a woman who has taken a vow.

Oberon. Give me that boy.

Titania. Not for thy fairy kingdom. Fairies, away!

Titania exits with her train.

Oberon. Well, go thy way. Thou shalt not from this grove
Till I torment thee for this injury.
My gentle Puck, come hither.
Fetch me that flow'r; the herb I showed thee once:
The juice of it on sleeping eyelids laid
Will make or man or woman° madly dote
Upon the next live creature that it sees.
Fetch me this herb.

Puck. I'll put a girdle round about the earth in forty
minutes. (*Puck exits.*)

Oberon. Having once this juice,
I'll watch Titania when she is asleep,
And drop the liquor of it in her eyes.
The next thing then she waking looks upon,
Be it on lion, bear, or wolf, or bull,
On meddling monkey, or on busy° ape,
She shall pursue it with the soul of love.
And ere I take this charm from off her sight,
As I can take it with another herb,
I'll make her render up her page to me.
But who comes here? I am invisible,
And I will overhear their conference.

Or man or woman: either man or woman.   *Busy:* meddlesome.

14

Enter Demetrius, followed by Helena.

Demetrius. I love thee not. Therefore pursue me not.
  Where is Lysander and fair Hermia?
  The one I'll slay, the other slayeth me.
  Thou told'st me they were stol'n unto this wood.

Helena. You draw me, you hardhearted adamant.°

Demetrius. Do I entice you? Do I speak you fair?°
  Or rather, do I not, in plainest truth
  Tell you I do not nor I cannot love you?

Helena. And even for that I do love you the more.
  I am your spaniel. Spurn me, strike me,
  Neglect me, lose me; only give me leave
  Unworthy as I am, to follow you.

Demetrius. Tempt not too much the hatred of my spirit,
  For I am sick when I do look on thee.

Helena. And I am sick when I look not on you.

Demetrius. You do impeach° your modesty too much,
  To leave the city, and commit yourself
  Into the hands of one that loves you not.

Helena. (Holding on to him.) Your virtue is my privilege.°

Adamant: stone.   *Speak you fair:* speak kindly to you.   *Impeach:* expose.
Virtue is my privilege: perfection is my reason.

Demetrius. Let me go!
Or, if thou follow me, do not believe
But I shall do thee mischief in the wood.

He exits.

Helena. I'll follow thee, and make a heaven of hell,
To die upon° the hand I love so well. (*She exits.*)

Oberon. Fare thee well, nymph. Ere he do leave this grove,
Thou shalt fly him, and he shall seek thy love.

Enter Puck.

Oberon. Has thou the flower there? Welcome, wanderer.

Puck. Ay, there it is.

Oberon. I pray thee, give it me.
I know a bank where the wild thyme blows,
Where the oxlips and the nodding violet grows,
Quite overcanopied with luscious woodbine,
With sweet musk roses, and with eglantine.
There sleeps Titania sometime of the night,
Lulled in these flowers with dances and delight;
And there the snake throws° her enameled skin,
Weed° wide enough to wrap a fairy in.

To die upon: dying by.   *Throws:* sheds.   *Weed:* garment.

16

Oberon. And with the juice of this I'll streak her eyes,
   And make her full of hateful fantasies.
   Take thou some of it, and seek through this grove.
   A sweet Athenian lady is in love
   With a disdainful youth. Anoint his eyes;
   But do it when the next thing he espies
   May be the lady. Thou shalt know the man
   By the Athenian garments he hath on.
   Effect it with some care that he may prove
   More fond on her° than she upon her love:
   And look thou meet me ere the first cock crow.

Puck. Fear not, my lord, your servant shall do so.

Puck hurries off and Oberon follows.

More fond on her: foolishly in love.

17

ACT II, SCENE 2.
ANOTHER PART OF THE WOODS.

Enter Titania with her train.

Titania. Come, now a roundel° and a fairy song.
Sing me asleep and let me rest.

Titania lays down as fairies sing and dance around her.

Peaseblossom. You spotted snakes with double tongue,
Thorny hedgehogs, be not seen.

Moth. Newts and blindworms° do no wrong,
Come not near our Fairy Queen.

All Fairies. Nightingale, with melody
Sing in our sweet lullaby;
Lulla, lulla, lullaby, lulla, lulla, lullaby:
Never harm nor spell nor charm,
Come our lovely lady nigh;
So good night with lullaby.

Cobweb. Weaving spiders come not here;
Hence, you long-legged spinners, hence!

Mustardseed. Beetles black, approach not near; worm nor
snail, do no offense.

All Fairies. (Repeat chorus.) Nightingale with melody...

Roundel: dance in a ring-actors will enjoy creating their own melody and dance
choreography.   *Blindworms:* small snakes.

Moth. Hence, away!

Cobweb. Now all is well.

Moth. One aloof stand sentinel.

Fairies exit as Oberon enters and squeezes the flower on Titania's eyelids.

Oberon. What thou seest when thou dost wake,
  Do it for thy truelove take;
  Love and languish for his sake.
  Be it lynx, or cat, or bear,
  Leopard, or boar with bristled hair,
  In thy eye that shall appear
  When thou wak'st, it is thy dear.
  Wake when some vile thing is near.

Oberon exits as Lysander and Hermia enter.

Lysander. Fair love, you faint with wand'ring in the wood;
  And to speak truth, I have forgot our way.
  We'll rest us, Hermia, if you think it good,
  And tarry for the comfort of the day.

Hermia. Be't so, Lysander. Find you out a bed;
  For I upon this bank will rest my head. *(She lies down.)*

Lysander. (He lies next to her.) One turf shall serve as
  pillow for us both,
  One heart, one bed, two bosoms, and one troth.°

Troth: pledged faith.

Hermia. (Rising.) Nay, good Lysander. *(He rises.)*
    For my sake, my dear,
    Lie further off yet,
    do not lie so near.

Lysander. O, take the sense,° sweet, of my innocence!

Hermia. Gentle friend, for love and courtesy,
    Lie further off, in human modesty.
    Such separation as may well be said
    Becomes a virtuous bachelor and a maid,
    So far be distant; and, good night, sweet friend.
    Thy love ne'er alter till thy sweet life end!

Lysander. Amen, amen, to that fair prayer, say I,
    And then end life when I end loyalty!
    Here is my bed. Sleep give thee all his rest!

They each lie down to sleep as Puck enters.

Puck. Who is here?
    Weeds° of Athens he doth wear:
    This is he, my master said,
    Despised the Athenian maid, and here the maiden,
    sleeping sound, on the dank and dirty ground. Pretty
    soul! She durst not lie near this lack-love, this kill cour-
    tesy. Churl,° upon thy eyes I throw all the power this
    charm doth owe. °

Take the sense: understand the true meaning.   *Weeds:* garments.
Churl: ill-mannered person.   *Owe:* possess.

20

Puck. When thou wak'st, let love forbid
  Sleep his seat on thy eyelid.
  So awake when I am gone,
  For I must now to Oberon.

*Puck exits as Demetrius and Helena enter, running, and
out of breath.*

Helena. Stay, though thou kill me, sweet Demetrius.

Demetrius. I charge thee, hence, and do not haunt me
  thus. I alone will go.

He exits. Helena is about to follow but notices Lysander.

Helena. But who is here? Lysander! On the ground!
  Dead? Or asleep? I see no blood, no wound.
  Lysander, if you live, good sir, awake.

Lysander. (Awaking.) And run through fire I will for thy
  sweet sake.
  Transparent° Helena! Nature shows art,
  That through thy bosom makes me see thy heart.
  Where is Demetrius? O, how fit a word
  Is that vile name to perish on my sword!

Helena. Do not say so, Lysander. Say not so.
  Hermia still loves you. Then be content.

Transparent: bright.

21

Lysander. Content with Hermia! No, I do repent
   The tedious minutes I with her have spent.
   Not Hermia, but Helena I love;
   Who will not change a raven for a dove?

Helena. Wherefore was I to this keen mockery born?
   When at your hands did I deserve this scorn?
   O, that a lady, of one man refused,
   Should of another therefore be abused!

She exits.

Lysander. She sees not Hermia. Hermia, sleep thou there,
   And never mayst thou come Lysander near!
   For as a surfeit of the sweetest things
   The deepest loathing to the stomach brings.
   O, to honor Helena and be her knight.

He exits as Hermia awakes.

Hermia. Help me, Lysander, help me! Do thy best
   To pluck this crawling serpent from my breast!
   Aye me, for pity! What a dream was here!
   Lysander, look how I do quake with fear.
   Methought a serpent eat° my heart away,
   And you sat smiling at his cruel prey. °
   Lysander! What, removed? Lysander! Lord!
   What, out of hearing? Gone? No sound, no word?
   Either death or you I'll find immediately.

Eat: Ate (pronounced "et").   *Prey:* preying.

22

THE WOOD.
Titania is asleep. Enter the clowns
(Quince, Snug, Bottom, Flute, Snout, and Starveling).

Quince. Pat,° pat; and here's a marvail's ° convenient
place for our rehearsal. We will do it in action as we will
do it before the Duke.

Bottom. Peter Quince?

Quince. What sayest thou, Bully° Bottom?

Bottom. There are things in this comedy of Pyramus and
Thisby that will never please. First, Pyramus must draw
a sword to kill himself; which the ladies cannot abide.
How answer you that?

Snout. By our lady, a perilous fear.

Starveling. I believe we must leave the killing out,
when all is done.

Bottom. Not a whit. I have a device to make all well. Write
me a prologue, and let the prologue seem to say, we will
do no harm with our swords, and that Pyramus is not
killed indeed; and, for the more better assurance, tell
them that I Pyramus am not Pyramus, but Bottom the
weaver. This will put them out of fear.

Snout. Will not the ladies be afeared of the lion?

Starveling. I fear it, I promise you!

Pat: perfect!   *Marvail's:* marvelous.   *Bully:* good fellow.

25

Snout. Then another prologue must tell he is not a lion.

Bottom: Nay, you must name his name, and half his face
must be seen through the lion's neck, and he himself
must speak, saying thus, "Ladies"... or, "Fair ladies...
I would wish you"... or, "I would request you"...or,
"I would entreat you...not to fear, not to tremble:
I am a man as other men are."

Quince. Well, it shall be so. But there is two hard things;
that is to bring the moonlight into a chamber; for, you
know, Pyrarmus and Thisby meet by moonlight.

Snout. Doth the moon shine that night we play our play?

Bottom. A calendar, a calendar! Look in the almanac; find
out moonshine, find out moonshine.

Quince. (Pulls out a very tiny book, thumbs through it.)
Yes, it doth shine that night.

Bottom. Why then, may you leave a casement of the great
chamber window, where we play, open, and the moon
may shine in at the casement.

Quince. Aye, or else one must come in with a bush of
thorns° and a lantern, and say he comes to disfigure,° or
to present, the person of Moonshine.

Thorns: English peasants believed in a legend where "the man in the moon"
gathered firewood on Sunday.   *Disfigure:* prefigure or present beforehand.

Bottom. Then, there is another thing. We must have a wall
in the great chamber; for Pyramus and Thisby, says the
story, did talk through the chink of a wall.

Snout. You can never bring in a wall. What say you,
Bottom?

Bottom. Some man or other must present Wall. Let him
hold his fingers thus, and through that cranny shall
Pyramus and Thisby whisper.

Quince. If that may be, then all is well. Come, sit down,
every mother's son, and rehearse your parts. Pyramus,
you begin. When you have spoken your speech, enter
into that brake. And so everyone according to his cue.

Enter Puck.

Puck. What hempen homespuns° have we swagg'ring here?
So near the cradle of the Fairy Queen? *(Sees them prepare
to rehearse.)* What, a play toward! ° I'll be an auditor; an
actor too perhaps, if I see cause.

Quince. Speak, Pyramus. Thisby, stand forth.

Pyramus. (Bottom.) Thisby, the flowers of odious savors
sweet...

Quince. Odors, odors.

Hempen homespuns: crude, coarse fellows.   *Toward:* in preparation.

Pyramus Odors savor sweet.
  So hath thy breath, my dearest Thisby dear.
    But hark, a voice! Stay thou but here awhile,
  And by and by° I will to thee appear. (*He exits.*)

Thisby (Flute). Must I speak now?

Quince. Ay, marry, must you. For you must understand he goes but to see a noise that he heard, and is to come again.

Thisby. Most radiant Pyramus, most lily-white of hue,
  Of color like the red rose on triumphant briar,
  I'll meet thee, Pyramus, at Ninny's tomb.°

Quince. "Ninus' tomb," man. Why, you must not speak that yet. That you answer to Pyramus. You speak all your part at once, cues and all. Pyramus enter. (*Waits.*) (*Calling offstage.*) Your cue is past.

Bottom enters with an ass's head.

Pyramus. If I were fair, Thisby, I were only thine.

Quince. O monstrous! O strange! We are haunted. Pray, masters! Fly, masters! Help!

Exit all the clowns but Bottom.

By and by: shortly.   *Ninny's tomb:* Ninus was the legendary founder of Ninevah.

Bottom. Why do they run away? This is a knavery of them
    to make me afeard.
    I will walk up and down here, and will sing, that they
    shall hear I am not afraid. *(He sings.)*

        The woosel cock° so black of hue,
            With orange-tawny bill,
        The throstle with his note so true,
            The wren with little quill°...

Titania. (Awaking.) What angel wakes me from my
    flow'ry bed?

Bottom. (Still singing.) The finch, the sparrow, and the lark,
        The plain song cuckoo gray,
            Whose note full many a man doth mark,
        And dares not answer nay...

Titania. I pray thee, gentle mortal, sing again.
    Mine ear is much enamored of thy note;
    So is mine eye enthralled to thy shape;
    And thy fair virtue's force perforce doth move me
    On the first view to say, to swear, I love thee.

Bottom. Me thinks, mistress, you should have little reason
    for that. And yet, to say the truth, reason and love keep
    little company nowadays.

Titania. Thou art as wise as thou art beautiful.

Woosel cock: black bird.   *Quill:* piping voice (pipe made from a hollow stalk).

Bottom. Not so, neither.

Titania. O, I do love thee. Therefore, go with me.
I'll give thee fairies to attend on thee,
And they shall fetch thee jewels from the deep,
And sing, while thou on pressed flowers dost sleep:
And I will purge thy mortal grossness so,
That thou shalt like an airy spirit go.
Peaseblossom! Cobweb! Moth! ° And Mustardseed!

Enter four fairies.

Peaseblossom. Ready.

Cobweb.   And I.

Moth.   And I.

Mustardseed.   And I.

All. Where shall we go?

Titania. Be kind and courteous to this gentleman;
Hop in his walks, and gambol in his eyes;
Feed him with apricots and blackberries,
With purple grapes, green figs, and mulberries;
The honeybags steal from the bumblebees.
Nod to him, elves, and do him courtesies.

Moth: pronounced mote.

Peaseblossom. Hail, mortal!

Cobweb.   Hail!

Moth.   Hail!

Mustardseed.   Hail!

Titania. Come, wait upon him. Lead him to my bower.

Titania and Bottom exit as they follow the dancing fairies, bringing the first scene of Act III to a close.

ACT III, SCENE 2.
ANOTHER PART OF THE WOODS.

Enter Oberon.

Oberon. I wonder if Titania be awaked,
 Then, what it was that next came in her eye,
 Which she must dote on in extremity.°
 Here comes my messenger. How now, mad spirit!

Puck enters.

Puck. My mistress with a monster is in love.
 Near to her close° and consecrated bower,
 While she was in her dull and sleeping hour,
 A crew of patches,° rude mechanicals,°
 That work for bread upon Athenian stalls,
 Were met together to rehearse a play,
 Intended for great Theseus' nuptial day.
 I led them on in this distracted fear,
 And left sweet Pyramus translated there:
 When in that moment, so it came to pass,
 Titania waked, and straightway loved an ass.

Oberon. This falls out better than I could devise.
 But has thou yet latched° the Athenian eyes
 With the love juice, as I did bid thee do?

Extremity: to the utmost degree.   *Close:* secret.   *Patches:* fools or clowns.
Latched: fastened.   *Rude mechanicals:* uneducated working men.

34

Puck. I took him sleeping...that is finished too...
  And the Athenian woman by his side;
  That, when he waked, of force° she must be eyed.

Enter Demetrius and Hermia.

Oberon. Stand close.° This is the same Athenian.

Puck. This is the woman, but not this the man.

Demetrius. O, why rebuke you him that loves you so?
  Lay breath so bitter on your bitter foe.

Hermia. Now I but chide; but I should use thee worse,
  For thou, I fear, hast given me cause to curse.
  If thou hast slain Lysander in his sleep,
  Being o'er shoes and blood, plunge in the deep,
  And kill me too.

Demetrius. I am not guilty of Lysander's blood,
  Nor is he dead, for aught that I can tell.

Hermia. I pray thee, tell me then that he is well.

Demetrius. An if I could, what should I get therefore?°

Hermia. A privilege, never to see me more.
  And from thy hated presence part I so.
  See me no more, whether he be dead or no. *(She exits.)*

Of force: by necessity.   *Close:* concealed.   *Therefore:* in return.

35

Demetrius. There is no following her in this fierce vein.
Here therefore for a while I will remain.

Demetrius lies down and sleeps.

Oberon. What hast thou done? Thou hast mistaken quite,
And laid the lovejuice on some truelove's sight.
About the wood go swifter than the wind,
And Helena of Athens look thou find.
All fancy-sick° she is and pale of cheer,°
With sighs of love, that costs the fresh blood dear:
By some illusion see thou bring her here.
I'll charm his eyes against she do appear. °

Puck. I go, I go; look how I go,
Swifter than arrow from the tartar's bow. *(He exits.)*

Oberon. Flower of this purple dye,
Hit with Cupid's archery,
Sink in apple of his eye.
When his love he doth espy,
Let her shine as gloriously
As the Venus of the sky.
When thou wak'st, if she be by,
Beg of her for remedy.

Enter Puck.

Fancy-sick: lovesick.   *Cheer:* face.   *Against she do appear:* in preparation
for her coming.

Puck. Captain of our fairy band,
  Helena is here at hand;
  And the youth, mistook by me,
  Pleading for a lover's fee.
  Shall we their fond pageant° see?
  Lord, what fools these mortals be!

Oberon. Stand aside. The noise they make
  Will cause Demetrius to awake.

Puck. Then will two at once woo one;
  That must needs be sport alone;°
  And those things do best please me
  That befall prepost'rously.

Enter Lysander and Helena.

Lysander. Why should you think that I should woo in
  scorn? Demetrius loves her, and he loves not you.

Demetrius. (Awakening.) O Helen, goddess, nymph,
    perfect, divine!
  To what, my love, shall I compare thine eyne?
  Crystal is muddy. O, how ripe in show°
  Thy lips, those kissing cherries, tempting grow!
  Let me kiss this princess, this seal of bliss!

Fond pageant: foolish exhibition.   *Alone:* unique.   *Show:* appearance.

37

Helena. O spite! O hell! I see you all are bent
To set against me for your merriment.
If you were civil° and knew courtesy,
You would not do me this much injury.
Can you not hate me, as I know you do,
But you must join in souls to mock me too?
O what derision! None of noble sort
Would so offend a virgin, and extort°
A poor soul's patience, all to make you sport.

Lysander. You are unkind, Demetrius. Be not so;
For you love Hermia; this you know I know.
And here, with all good will, with all my heart,
In Hermia's love I yield you up my part;
And yours of Helena to me bequeath,
Whom I do love, and will do till my death.

Helena. Never did mockers waste more idle breath.

Demetrius. Lysander, keep thy Hermia; I will none.
If e'er I loved her, all that love is gone.

Lysander.   Helen, it is not so.

Demetrius. Look, where thy love comes; yonder is thy
dear.

Enter Hermia.

Hermia. Why unkindly didst thou leave me so?

Civil: civilized.   *Extort:* torture.

38

Lysander. Why should he stay, whom love doth press to
   go?

Hermia. What love could press Lysander from my side?

Lysander. Why seek'st thou me? Could not this make thee
   know,
  the hate I bare thee made me leave thee so?

Hermia. You speak not as you think. It cannot be.

Helena. Lo, she is one of this confederacy!
  Now I perceive they have conjoined all three
  To fashion this false sport, in spite of me.
  Injurious° Hermia! Most ungrateful maid!
  Have you conspired, have you with these contrived
  To bait° me with this foul derision?

Hermia. I am amazed at your passionate words.
  I scorn you not. It seems that you scorn me.

Helena. Have you not set Lysander, as in scorn,
  To follow me and praise my eyes and face?
  And made your other love, Demetrius,
  To call me goddess, nymph, divine and rare,
  Precious, celestial?

Hermia. I understand not what you mean by this.

Injurious: insulting.　*Bait:* torment.

39

Helena. Aye, do! Perserver,° counterfeit sad looks,°
   Make mouths° upon me when I turn my back;
   Wink at each other; hold the sweet jest up.
   This sport, well carried, shall be chronicled.
   If you have any pity, grace or manners,
   You would not make me such an argument.°
   But fare ye well. 'Tis partly my own fault,
   Which death or absence soon shall remedy.

Lysander. Stay, gentle Helena; hear my excuse.
   My love, my life, my soul, fair Helena!

Helena. O excellent!

Lysander. Helen, I love thee; by my life, I do!
   I swear by that which I will lose for thee,
   To prove him false that says I love thee not.

Demetrius. I say I love thee more than he can do.

Lysander. If thou say so, withdraw and prove it too.

Hermia. Why are you grown so rude! What change is this,
   Sweet love?

Lysander.   Thy love! Out, tawny Tartar, out!
   Out, loathed med'cine! O hated potion, hence!

Lysander is about to strike Hermia but stops himself.

Perserver: persevere with accent on the second syllable.   *Counterfeit sad looks:*
serious looks.   *Mouths:* mocking faces.   *Argument:* subject (of scorn).

Lysander. What, should I hurt her, strike her, kill her dead?
Although I hate her, I'll not harm her so.

Hermia. What, can you do me greater harm than hate?
Hate me? Wherefore? O me! What news, my love!
Am not I Hermia? Are not you Lysander?
I am as fair now as I was erewhile. °

Lysander.   'Tis no jest
That I do hate thee, and love Helena.

Hermia. O me! You juggler! You canker blossom! °
You thief of love!

Helena. You counterfeit. You puppet, you!

Hermia.   Puppet? Why so?
Because I am so dwarfish and so low?
How low am I, thou painted maypole? Speak!
How low am I? I am not yet so low
but that my nails can reach unto thine eyes.

Helena. (Hides behind one of the men.)
I pray you, though you mock me, gentlemen,
Let her not hurt me. I was never curst;°
I have no gift at all in shrewishness;

Hermia. Why get you gone. Who is't that hinders you?

Erewhile: a little while ago.   *Canker blossom:* worm that destroys the bud.
Curst: sharp-tongued.

41

Helena. Though she be little, she is fierce.

Hermia. "Little" again! Nothing but "low" and "little!"
Why will you suffer her to flout me thus?
Let me come to her. *(She tries to reach Helena.)*

Lysander. Get you gone, you dwarf,
You minimus,°of hind'ring knotgrass° made,
You bead, you acorn!

Demetrius. Let her alone. Speak not of Helena,
Take not her part; for, if thou dost intend°
Never so little show of love to her,
Thou shalt aby° it.

Lysander.   Now she holds me not.
Now follow, if thou dar'st, to try whose right,
Of thine or mine, is most in Helena.

Demetrius. Follow! Nay, I'll go with thee, cheek by jowl.

Lysander and Demetrius exit.

Hermia. You, mistress, all this coil is 'long of you.°
Nay, go not back.

Helena.   I will not trust you, I,
Nor longer stay in your curst company.
Your hands than mine are quicker for a fray,
My legs are longer though, to run away.

Minimus: tiny creature.   *Knotgrass:* a weed that can stunt the growth of
animals or children.   *Intend:* offer or pretend.   *Aby:* pay for.
This coil is 'long of you: All this turmoil is brought about by you.

42

Hermia. I am amazed,° and know not what to say.

Helena and Hermia exit.

Oberon. This is thy negligence. Still thou mistak'st, or else
committ'st thy knaveries willfully.

Puck. Believe me, king of shadows, I mistook.
Did not you tell me I should know the man
By the Athenian garments he had on?

Oberon. Thou sees these lovers seek a place to fight.
Hie therefore, Robin overcast the night;
Then crush this herb into Lysander's eye,
Whose liquor hath this virtuous° property,
To take from thence all error with his might,
And make his eyeballs roll with wonted sight.
When they next wake, all this derision°
Shall seem a dream and fruitless vision,
And back to Athens shall the lovers wend,
With league whose date° till death shall never end.
Whiles I in this affair do thee employ,
I'll to my queen and beg her Indian boy;
And then I will charmed eye release
From monster's view, and all things shall be peace.

Puck. My fairy lord, this must be done with haste,
For night's swift dragons cut the clouds full fast,
And yonder shines Aurora's harbinger,°
At whose approach, ghosts, wand'ring here and there,
troop home to the churchyards

Amazed: confused.   *Virtuous:* powerful.   *Derision:* laughable mockery.
Date: duration.   *Harbinger:* the precursor of dawn, the morning star.

Oberon. But we are spirits of another sort.
                         Haste; make no delay.
    We may effect this business yet ere day.

Oberon exits.

Puck. Upon and down, up and down,
    I will lead them up and down:
    I am feared in field and town:
    Goblin,° lead them up and down.
    Here comes one.

Enter Lysander.

Lysander. Where art thou, proud Demetrius? Speak thou
    now.

Puck. Here, villain; drawn° and ready. Where art thou?

Lysander. I will be with thee straight.

Puck.   Follow me, then. To plainer°
    ground.

Lysander exit and enter Demetrius.

Demetrius.   Lysander! Speak again!
    Thou runaway, thou coward, art thou fled?
    Speak! In some bush? Where dost thou hide thy head?

Goblin: one of Puck's names.   *Drawn:* with sword drawn.   *Plainer:* more level.

Puck. Thou coward, art thou bragging to the stars,
  Telling the bushes that thou look'st for wars,
  And wilt not come? Come, recreant! Come, thou child!
  I'll whip thee with a rod. He is defiled
  That draws a sword on thee.

Demetrius. Yea, art thou here?

Puck. Follow my voice. We'll try no manhood° here.

Puck exits.

Lysander. He goes before me and still dares me on:
  I followed fast, but faster he did fly,
  That fallen am I in dark uneven way,
  And here will rest me. *(Lies down.)*
    Come thou gentle day!
  For if but once thou show me thy gray light,
  I'll find Demetrius, and revenge this spite. *(He sleeps.)*

Enter Puck and Demetrius.

Puck. Ho, ho, ho! Coward, why com'st thou not?

Demetrius. Where art thou now?

Puck.   Come hither. I am here.

Demetrius. Nay, then, thou mock'st me. Thou shalt buy
  this dear,° if ever I thy face by daylight see. *(He sleeps.)*

Try no manhood: have no test of valor.   *Buy this dear:* pay dearly for this.

Puck. On the ground
Sleep sound.
I'll apply
To your eye,
Gentle lover, remedy.

He squeezes the juice on Lysander's eye.

When thou wak'st,
Thou tak'st
True delight
In the sight
Of thy former lady's eye.
And the country proverb known,
That every man should take his own,
In your waking shall be shown.
Jack shall have Jill,
Nought shall go ill;
The man shall have his mare again, and all shall be well.

Act III is concluded as Puck exits.

Actor / Director Notes

Actor / Director Notes

THE WOOD.

Lysander, Demetrius, Hermia and Helena are all asleep.
Enter Titania, fairies, Bottom, and Oberon.

Titania. Come, sit thee down upon this flow'ry bed,
   While I thy amiable cheeks do coy,°
   And stick musk roses in thy sleek smooth head,
   And kiss thy fair large ears, my gentle joy.

Bottom. Where's Peaseblossom?

Peaseblossom. Ready.

Bottom. Scratch my head, Peaseblossom. Where's
   Mounsieur Cobweb?

Cobweb. Ready.

Bottom. Mounsieur Cobweb, good mounsieur, get you
   your weapons in your hand, and kill me a red-hipped
   humblebee on the top of a thistle; and, good mounsieur,
   bring me the honey bag. Where's mounsieur
   Mustardseed?

Mustardseed. What's your will?

Bottom. Nothing, good mounsieur, but to help Cavalery°
   Cobweb to scratch. I must to the barber's, mounsieur;
   for methinks I am marvail's° hairy about the face and I
   am such a tender ass, if my hair do but tickle me, I must
   scratch.

While I do coy: while I caress your lovely cheeks.   *Cavalery:* cavalier, addressing a
man of fashion.   *Marvail's:* marvelous.

Titania. O say, sweet love, what thou desirest to eat?

Bottom. I could munch your good dry oats. Methinks I
have a great desire to a bottle° of hay. Good hay, sweet
hay, hath no fellow.°

Titania. I have a venturous fairy that shall seek
The squirrel's hoard, and fetch thee new nuts.

Bottom. I pray you, let none of your people disturb me. I
have an exposition of° sleep come upon me.

Titania. Sleep thou, and I will wind thee in my arms.
Fairies, be gone, and be all ways° away. *(Fairies exit.)*
So doth the woodbine the sweet honeysuckle
Gently entwist; the female ivy so
Enrings the barky fingers of the elm.
O, how I love thee! How I dote on thee.

They sleep as Puck enters.

Oberon. Welcome, good Robin. See'st thou this sweet
sight?
Her dotage now I do begin to pity.
I did ask of her changeling child;
Which straight she gave me, and her fairy sent
To bear him to my bower in fairy land.

Bottle: bundle.   *Fellow:* equal.   *Exposition of:* disposition for.
All ways away: in every direction.

Oberon. And now I have the boy, I will undo
  This hateful imperfection of her eyes,
  And, gentle Puck, take this transformed scalp
  From off the head of this Athenian swain,°
  That he awaking when the other° do,
  May all to Athens back again repair,
  And think no more of this night's accidents,°
  But as the fierce vexation of a dream.
  But first I will release the Fairy Queen.
    Be as thou wast wont to be;
    See as thou wast wont to see.
    Dian's bud o'er Cupid's flower
    Hath such force and blessed power.
  Now, my Titania, wake you, my sweet Queen.

Titania. My Oberon, what visions I have seen!
  Methought I was enamored of an ass.

Oberon. There lies your love.

Titania.   How came these things to pass?
  O, mine eyes do loathe his visage now!

Oberon. Silence awhile. Robin, take off his head.
  Now thou and I are new in amity,
  And will tomorrow midnight solemnly°
  Dance in Duke Theseus' house triumphantly,°
  And bless it to all fair prosperity.
  There shall the pairs of faithful lovers be
  Wedded, with Theseus, all in jollity.

Swain: young man in love.   *Other:* others.   *Accidents:* incidents.
Solemnly: ceremoniously.   *Triumphantly:* in festive procession.

Puck. Fairy King, attend, and mark.
       I do hear the morning lark.

Oberon. Then, my Queen, in silence sad,°
       Trip we after night's shade.
       We the globe can compass soon,
       Swifter than the wand'ring moon.

Titania. Come, my lord; and in our flight,
       Tell me how it came this night,
       That I sleeping here was found
       With these mortals on the ground.

They exit as Theseus, Hippolyta and Egeus enter.

Theseus. My hounds are bred out of the Spartan kind,°
       So flewed, so sanded;° and their heads are hung
       With ears that sweep away the morning dew.
       But soft! ° What nymphs are these?

Egeus. My lord, this is my daughter here asleep;
       And this, Lysander; this Demetrius is;
       This Helena, old Nedar's Helena.
       I wonder of their being here together.

Theseus. No doubt they rose up early to observe the rite of
       May, and, hearing our intent, came here in grace of our
       solemnity. ° But speak, Egeus. Is not this the day that
       Hermia should give answer of her choice?

Sad: serious.   Spartan hounds: famous for their hunting skills.   *Sanded:* of
sandy color.   *Soft:* stop.   *In grace of our solemnity:* in honor of this festival.

Egeus. It is, my lord.

They all awake.

Lysander. Pardon, my lord.

Theseus.   I pray you all, stand up.
  I know you two are rival enemies.
  How comes this gentle concord in the world?

Lysander. I came with Hermia hither. Our intent
  Was to be gone from Athens, where we might,
  Without the peril of°the Athenian law—

Egeus. Enough, enough, my lord; you have enough.
  I beg the law, the law, upon his head.
  They would have stol'n away!

Demetrius. My lord, fair Helena told me of their stealth, °
  Of this their purpose hither to this wood,
  And I in fury hither followed them,
  Fair Helena in fancy° following me.
  But, my good lord, I wot not by what power...
  But by some power it is...my love to Hermia,
  Melted as the snow.
  But now I do wish it, love it, long for it,
  And will forevermore be true to it.

Without the peril: beyond the dangerous reach.   *Stealth:* stealthy flight.
Fancy: love.

Theseus. Fair lovers, you are fortunately met.
Of this discourse we more will hear anon.°
Egeus, I will overbear your will,
For in the temple, by and by,° with us
These couples shall eternally be knit.
Away with us to Athens! Three and three,
We'll hold a feast in great solemnity.
Come, all!

Theseus, Hippolyta and Egeus exit.

Hermia. Methinks I see things with parted eye,°
When everything seems double.

Helena. And I have found Demetrius like a jewel,
Mine own, and not mine own.

Demetrius.   Are you sure
That we are awake? It seems to me
That yet we sleep, we dream. Do not you think
The Duke was here, and bid us follow him?

Hermia. Yea, and my father.

Helena. And Hippolyta.

Lysander. And he did bid us follow to the temple.

Demetrius. Why then, we are awake. Let's follow him,
And by the way let us recount our dreams. (*They exit.*)

Anon: soon, in a little while.   *By and by:* shortly.   *Parted eye:* blurred vision.

54

Bottom. (Awaking.) When my cue comes, call me,
and I will answer. My next is, "My most fair Pyramus."
Heigh-ho!° Peter Quince? Snout, the tinker? Starveling?
G-d's my life,° stol'n hence, and left me asleep? I have
had a most rare vision. I have had a dream. Man is but
an ass if he go about to expound this dream. Methought
I was...there is no man can tell what. Methought I
was... and methought I had...but man is but a patched°
fool if he will offer to say what methought I had. The eye
of man hath not heard, the ear of man hath not seen,
man's hand is not able to taste, his tongue to conceive,
nor his heart to report, what my dream was. I will get
Peter Quince to write a ballet° of this dream. It shall be
called "Bottom's dream," because it hath no bottom; and
I will sing it in the latter end of a play, before the Duke.
Peradventure to make it the more gracious,° I shall sing
it at her° death.

He exits.

Heigh-ho!: a yawn.   *Patched:* referring to the patchwork dress of jesters.
Ballet: ballad.   *Gracious:* attractive.   *Her:* Thisby's.

55

ACT V, SCENE 1.

ATHENS. THE PALACE OF THESEUS.

Theseus, Hippolyta, Philostrate, and possible attendants.

Hippolyta. 'Tis strange, my Theseus, that these lovers
   speak of.

Theseus. More strange than true. I never may believe
   These antique° fables, nor these fairy toys.°
   Here come the lovers, full of joy and mirth.
   Joy, gentle friends! Come. What masques?

Philostrate. A play there is, my lord, some ten words long,
   Which is as brief as I have known a play;
   But by ten words, my lord, it is too long,
   Which makes it tedious. For in all the play
   There is not one word apt, one player fitted.

Theseus. What are they that do play it?

Philostrate. Hard-handed men, that work in Athens here,
   Which never labored in their minds till now;
   And now have toiled their unbreathed° memories
   With this same play, against° your nuptial.

Theseus. We will hear it.

Philostrate. No, my noble lord.
   It is not for you. I have heard it over,
   And it is nothing, nothing in the world.

Antique: ancient   *Fairy toys:* trifling stories about fairies.
Unbreathed: unexercised.   *Against:* in preparation for.

58

Theseus.   I will hear that play.
  Go, bring them in, and take your places, ladies.

Exit Philostrate.

Hippolyta. I love not to see wretchedness o'ercharged,°
  And duty in his service perishing.

Theseus. Why, gentle sweet, you shall see no such thing.

Hippolyta. He says they can do nothing in this kind. °

Theseus. The kinder we, to give them thanks for nothing.
  Our sport shall be to take what they mistake.

Enter Philostrate.

Philostrate. So, please your Grace, the Prologue is
  addressed.°

Theseus. Let him approach. *(Trumpets flourish.)*

Enter the Prologue (Quince).

Prologue. If we offend, it is with our good will.
  That you should think, we come not to offend,
    But with good will. To show our simple skill,
  That is the true beginning of our end. °

Enter Pyramus and Wall.

Wretchedness o'ercharged: lowly people overburdened.   *In this kind:* in this kind
of thing (i.e., acting).   *Addressed:* ready.   *End:* aim.

Wall. In this same interlude it doth befall
   That I, one Snout by name, present a wall;
   And such a wall, as I would have you think,
   That had in it a crannied hole or chink,
   Through which the lovers, Pyramus and Thisby,
   Did whisper often very secretly.

Pyramus. O grim-looked night! O night with hue so black!
   O night, which ever art when day is not!
      O night, O night! Alack, alack, alack, I fear my
   Thisby's promise is forgot.
      And thou, O wall, O sweet, O lovely wall,
      That stand'st between her father's ground and mine!
      Thou wall, O wall, O sweet and lovely wall,
      Show me thy chink, to blink through with mine eyne

Wall holds up two fingers in the shape of scissors.

Pyramus. Thanks, courteous wall. Jove shield thee well
      for this!
   But what see I? No Thisby do I see.
      O wicked wall, through whom I see no bliss!
   Cursed be thy stones for thus deceiving me!

Theseus. The wall, methinks, being sensible,° should curse
   again.

Pyramus. No, in truth, sir, he should not. "Deceiving me" is
   Thisby's cue. She is to enter now, and I am to spy her
   through the wall. You shall see it will fall pat° as I told
   you. Yonder she comes.

Sensible: capable of feeling   *Fall pat:* happen exactly.

Enter Thisby.

Thisby. O wall, full often hast thou heard my moans,
    For parting my fair Pyramus and me! ·
My cherry lips have often kissed thy stones,
    thy stones with lime and hair knit up in thee.

Pyramus. I see a voice. Now will I to the chink,
  Thisby!

Thisby. My love thou art, my love I think.

Pyramus. O kiss me through the hole of this vile wall!

Thisby kisses wall's fingers.

Thisby. I kiss the wall's hole, not your lips at all.

Pyramus. Wilt thou to Ninny's tomb meet me straight
  away?

Thisby. 'Tide life, 'tide death,° I come without delay.

Pyramus and Thisby exit.

Wall. Thus have I, Wall, my part discharged so;
    And, being done, thus Wall away doth go.

Wall exits.

'Tide death: life or death.

Hippolyta. This is the silliest stuff that ever I heard.

Theseus. The best in this kind° are but shadows; and the worst are no worse, if imagination amend them.

Hippolyta. It must be your imagination then, and not theirs.

Theseus. If we imagine no worse of them than they of themselves, they may pass for excellent men. Here come two noble beasts in, a man and a lion.

Enter Lion and Moonshine.

Lion. You, ladies, you, whose gentle hearts do fear
The smallest monstrous mouse that creeps on floor,
May now perchance both quake and tremble here,
When lion rough in wildest rage doth roar. Then know
that I, as Snug the joiner, am
A lion fell,° nor else no lion's dam;
For, if I should as lion come in strife
Into this place, 'twere pity on my life.°

Theseus. A very gentle° beast, and of a good conscience.

Demetrius. The very best at a beast, my lord, that e'er I saw. Now, let us listen to the moon.

Moonshine. This lanthorn° doth the horned moon present.

In this kind: of this profession (i.e, actors).   *Lion fell:* fierce lion.   *Twere pity on my life:* dangerous thing for me.   *Gentle:* courteous.   *Lanthorn:* lantern.

Awkward pause.

Lysander. Proceed, Moon.

Moonshine. The lanthorn is the moon; i, the man i' th'
moon; this thorn bush, my thorn bush; and this dog, my
dog.

Demetrius. Here comes Thisby!

Enter Thisby.

Thisby. This is old Ninny's tomb. Where is my love?

Lion. Oh...

The lion roars and Thisby runs off.

Demetrius. Well roared, Lion.

Theseus. Well run, Thisby.

Hippolyta. Well shone, Moon. Truly, the moon shines
with a good grace.

The lion shakes Thisby's mantle and exits.

Theseus. Well shaken, Lion.

Enter Pyramus.

Pyramus. Sweet Moon, I thank thee for thy sunny beams;
  I thank thee, Moon, for shining now so bright;
  For by thy gracious, golden, glittering gleams,
    I trust to take of truest Thisby sight.
      But stay, O spite! °
      But mark, poor knight.
    What dreadful dole° is here!
    Eyes do you see?
    How can it be?
  O dainty duck! O dear!
    Thy mantle good,
    What, stained with blood!

Theseus. This passion, and the death of a dear friend,
  would go near to make a man look sad.

Hippolyta. Beshrew° my heart, but I pity the man.

Pyramus. O wherefore, Nature, didst thou lions frame?
  Since lion vile hath here deflow'red my dear:
    Which is...no, no...which was the fairest dame
  That lived, that loved, that liked, that looked with
  cheer.°
    Come, tears, confound:
    Out, sword and wound
  The pap of Pyramus;
    Ay, that left pap,
    Where heart doth hop. *(Stabs himself.)*
  Thus die I, thus, thus, thus.
  Now am I dead,

Spite: vexation. *Dole:* sorrowful thing. *Beshrew:* mild curse.
Cheer: countenance.

Pyramus. Now am I fled;
    My soul is in the sky.
        Tongue, lose thy light;
        Moon, take thy flight.

Exit Moonshine.

        Now die, die, die, die, die. *(He dies.)*

Hippolyta. How chance° moonshine is gone before
    Thisby comes back and finds her lover?

Theseus. She will find him by starlight. Here she comes;
    and her passion° ends the play.

Enter Thisby.

Thisby. Asleep, my love?
        What, dead, my dove?
      O Pyramus, arise!
        Speak, speak. Quite dumb?
        Dead, dead? A tomb
    Must cover thy sweet eyes.
        These lily lips,
        This cherry nose,
    These yellow cowslip cheeks,
        Are gone, are gone.
        Lovers, make moan.
        Tongue, not a word.
          Come, trusty sword.
    Come, blade, my breast imbrue! ° *(Stabs herself.)*

How chance: how does it come that.   *Passion:* passionate speech.
Imbrue: stain with blood.

Thisby.   And, farewell, friends.
Thus Thisby ends.
Adieu, adieu, adieu. *(He dies.)*

Theseus. Moonshine and Lion are left to bury the dead.

Demetrius. Aye, and Wall too.

Bottom. No, I assure you; the wall is down that parted
their fathers. Will it please you to see the epilogue, or to
hear a Bergomask dance° between two of our company?

Theseus. No epilogue, I pray you; for your play needs no
excuse.
The iron tongue of midnight hath told° twelve,
Lovers, to bed; 'tis almost fairy time.
I fear we shall outsleep the coming morn,
As much as we this night have overwatched.
This palpable-gross° play hath well beguiled
The heavy gait of night. Sweet friends, to bed.

*All exit one direction
as Puck enters from another with a broom.*

Bergomask dance: rustic dance.   *Told:* counted.   *Palpable-gross:* obviously
grotesque.

66

Puck. Now the hungry lion roars
  And the wolf behowls the moon;
    Now is the time of night,
  That the graves, all gaping wide,
    Everyone lets forth his sprite,°
  In the churchway paths to glide.
    And we fairies that do run
  From the presence of the sun.
    I am sent with broom, before,
  To sweep the dust behind the door. °

Oberon and Titania enter with all their train.

Oberon. Through the house give glimmering light,
  By the dead and drowsy fire:
    Every elf and fairy sprite
  Hop as light as bird from brier;
    And this ditty, after me,
    Sing, and dance it trippingly.

Titania. First, rehearse your song by rote,
  To each word a warbling note:
  Hand in hand, with fairy grace,
  Will we sing and bless this place.

All sing and dance.

Sprite: ghost.   *Behind the door:* Robin Goodfellow was a household spirit so he is
sent to clean the house before the king and queen arrive.

Oberon. Now, until the break of day
   Through this house each fairy stray.
   To the best bride-bed will we,
   Which by us shall blessed be.
   With this field-dew consecrate,
   Every fairy take his gait,°
   And each several° chamber bless
   Through this palace with sweet peace,
   And the owner of it blest
   Ever shall in safety rest.
   Trip away, make no stay,
   Meet me all by break of day.

All exit but Puck.

Puck. (Approaching the audience.) If we shadows have
      offended,
   Think but this, and all is mended,
   That you have but slumb'red here,
   While these visions did appear.
   And this weak and idle° theme,
   No more yielding but° a dream,
   Gentles, do not reprehend.
   If you pardon, we will mend.

Take his gait: proceed.   *Several:* individual.   *Idle:* foolish.
No more yielding: no more than.

68

Puck. And, as I am an honest Puck,
  If we have unearnèd luck
  Now to escape the serpent's tongue,°
  We will make amends ere long,
  Else the Puck a liar call.
  So, good night unto you all.
  Give me your hands,° if we be friends,
  And Robin shall restore amends.

He exits as the play comes to a finish.

Serpent's tongue: to escape hisses from the audience.   *Give me your hands:* applaud.

ADDITIONAL STAGING
CONSIDERATIONS

Scenery

Shakespeare staging typically contains an "upper above" (balcony) and "inner below" (stage floor). They permit the use of different levels and locations for actors to enter and exit. If that isn't an option, consider a few small-sized classroom acting boxes to add levels for standing and sitting. In *The Tempest*, for example, they would be helpful for Ariel, unseen by everyone but Prospero, to be in the midst of or behind the action. Adding levels will provide numerous options for blocking.

Pacing

Let's say one page in your script has ten different cues. If actors take three seconds before coming in with their lines, they will add thirty seconds *per page*. Ninety pages means, forty-five minutes where nothing is being said! Actors will often say, "But I need time to listen and formulate my response." Yes, in real life, but not in the theatre where we are typically "lifelike." Unless indicated otherwise, actors should take less than a second to come in with their lines. Work on pacing *after* they are solidly off book and remind them this is about picking up cues, *not* speeding their delivery. Trust me, audience members will appreciate the pace!

Actor / Director Notes

The introduction to SHAKESPEARE is not an easy task. Sometimes the magic can use a little assistance...

Don't Miss These Bestselling Books!

To make the works of Shakespeare accessible to all ages and levels of education, Cass Foster combines his experience as a professor emeritus of theatre, fight choreographer and stage director to provide *Shakespeare: To Teach or not to Teach*, *Shakespeare for Children*, and the *Sixty-Minute Shakespeare* series—judiciously condensed versions of the Bard's classics. Titles sold individually or as a set.